THE
PROMISE QUILT

THE PROMISE QUILT

CANDICE F. RANSOM

Illustrations by Ellen Beier

WALKER & COMPANY

NEW YORK

When I was little, Papa and I often leaned against the coffee tree to watch the sun set over Lost Mountain.

"When you are bigger, Addie, I'll take you to school on the other side of the ridge," Papa promised. "You'll learn to read and write and make your mark in this life."

Back then, my life was Papa and Mama and my older brother on our little farm tucked into the lap of Lost Mountain.

I thought the world ended over that rise.

And for five springs, it did.

War came to Virginia.

Men from faraway states marched off to fight for something called the Cause.

Papa stepped outside and met the war in his dooryard. He left one rainy day to be General Lee's guide.

The last thing I saw was his red flannel shirt.

The dull boom of distant cannons circled Lost Mountain like endless thunder. Sometimes shells whistled overhead.

Mama, Aldine, and I would hide under the kitchen table, holding hands and praying.

Soldiers tramped through our farm, blue coats and gray. They killed our pigs and chickens and took our fence posts for firewood.

Mama read us Papa's letters from places like Antietam Creek and Gettysburg. He wrote them on the backs of broadsides, his script cramped to save space.

The seasons dragged by.

Mama turned my dresses twice because we couldn't buy calico and tried to hide her tears when the army chopped down our coffee tree.

At last the war was over.

A neighbor told us that General Lee had surrendered to General Grant.

Every day, weary soldiers straggled past our farm on their way home.

But not Papa.

At first I thought he was lost, like the Cause everyone talked about.

Then we learned Papa had died in a Northern hospital. A lady from Pennsylvania sent Mama his red shirt. Mama gave it to me.

Aldine said we were poor.

"We still have each other," Mama told us. "We just don't have any money."

In Papa's tin box we found a stack of Confederate notes and a twenty-five-cent piece. The bills were worthless, but Mama bought a sack of corn with the silver coin.

My brother hitched himself to the plow. I dropped seed in his crooked rows, four grains to the hill.

One for the blackbird,
One for the crow,
One for the cutworm,
One to grow.

Papa had taught me that rhyme. I pushed the warm red dirt with my toes and thought of him.

We ate boiled turnip tops until the corn came in. Aldine scoured the charred countryside for stove wood.

I missed Papa more each day.

Yet Mama still sang her favorite hymn. "Beyond the sunset's radiant glow, there's a brighter world, I know."

I wondered if the world would ever be bright again.

When the corn crop was ready, Aldine and I toted a hefty bag to the gristmill.

Barren woods along the road showed blackened stumps like rotted teeth. One tree was so riddled with lead, it couldn't even be split for kindling.

The mill had been a hospital during the war.

I spied writing scratched on the damp stone walls.

"What are those words?" I asked the miller.

"The names of the wounded and dying," he said.

I traced rough-edged letters and wondered where Papa had left his mark.

That summer Aldine found a bee tree. We had wild honey to drizzle on our cornbread.

Mama and I picked the last of the blackberries, standing hipdeep in brambles. I wore Papa's shirt to keep from getting scratched.

At last it was time to go to school.

"There is no school," Mama told me. "The soldiers burned it."

"But Papa promised!" I cried. "He said I would go to school when I was bigger!"

Mama thought a moment. Then she said, "Maybe we'll find a way."

She met with our neighbors.

Mr. Brown would let us use his shed while the men rebuilt the schoolhouse. But we still needed books and slates.

Mama wrote to the lady in Pennsylvania who had sent Papa's things, asking if she knew how we could get books for our school.

The Pennsylvania lady replied that she'd be glad to help. If Mama would make a quilt, she would raffle it. The money could be used to buy books.

Mama dug out her ragbag and laid scraps in a checkerboard arrangement.

"This is a new pattern," she said. "It's called Lee's Surrender."

Night after night, she stitched on the quilt.
I sat on the rug and sleepily watched the needle dart
in and out. Soon we would have our books, and I
could go to school.

But one evening Mama set down her hoop.

"I don't have enough material for the border!" she
said. "I can't finish the quilt!"

I was snuggled in Papa's shirt, the only thing I had
to remember him by.

I couldn't give up Papa's shirt!

But then I realized the quilt wasn't just for me. It was for all the children who wanted to go to school and make their mark in this world.

Slowly I slipped off the shirt.

"Use this," I said.

"Addie, are you sure?" Mama asked me. "This is all we have left of Papa."

"We have memories," I said, and Aldine nodded.

Mama hugged me. "I promise to save you a little piece. Red will look nice mixed with the blue border."

She scissored Papa's shirt into strips. Then she picked out the stitches from the blue border and started over.

As she sewed, I watched the red shirt become part of the pattern.

I thought about Papa's promise. In a way, he was keeping it.

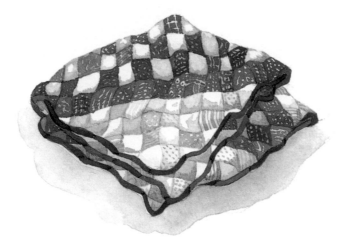

When the quilt was finished, Mama sent it to the lady in Pennsylvania. The quilt was raffled, the lady wrote to us. It fetched a good price.

One fine morning we received a box of books so new, the covers cracked when we opened them. I breathed in the wonderful smell of words yet unread.

On the first day of school, I hiked over Lost Mountain with Aldine.

On the other side, a stream of eager-faced children poured into Mr. Brown's shed.

No one minded sharing seats or using splintered boards nailed to the walls as desks.

Teacher had hung a tattered map of the United States to cover the bullet holes. She showed us Virginia, one state among many.

Later Teacher taught us how to print our names.

I stared at the letters on my new slate. I had finally made my mark in this bright, new world.

Papa would be proud.

The Civil War, April 1861 to April 1865, ripped apart the American Republic. Northern and Southern states were sharply divided on political issues involving slavery and states' rights.

The battle cry Southerners adopted was the Cause, the belief that they should be able to leave the Union and form their own government. Eleven states composed the Confederate States of America. Men were ready—even eager—for a confrontation with their Northern neighbors.

But the war was fought mainly on Southern soil. Battles ravaged farmland and woodland, small towns and big cities. Innocent women and children were caught in the path of devastation and destruction. Families either fled the fighting or stayed in their homes, facing danger. Everyone endured hardships.

Food, fuel, and daily necessities like soap and paper became scarce. Letters were penned on wallpaper, broadsides (advertisements), and even on other letters. The writer simply turned the page sideways and wrote across the script. Dresses and shirts were "twice-turned" to make them last. Garments were taken apart, then restitched inside-out.

Confederate general Robert E. Lee surrendered to Union general Ulysses S. Grant on April 9, 1865. The table on which Lee signed the document was rumored to have had a checkered top. (As soon as the two generals left the room, all furnishings were stolen or purchased for souvenirs.) We now know that the table was gray marble with a mahogany pedestal. (It's on display in the Chicago Historical Society.) Yet "Lee's Surrender," a checkerboard pattern, became a traditional quilt and coverlet design after the war.

Four years of fighting left an indelible mark on the nation. Nearly 500,000 Americans died in the conflict.

Peace and healing took a long time. War taught Americans a hard lesson.

Now the country once divided stands together, stronger than ever.

For Ruth, my favorite cousin
—C. R.
Affectionately, for Claire and Rachel
—E. B.

Thanks to Donald C. Pfanz, staff historian, Fredericksburg and
Spotsylvania National Military Park

Text copyright © 1999 by Candice F. Ransom
Illustrations copyright © 1999 by Ellen Beier

First published in the United States of America in 1999 by Walker Publishing Company, Inc.

Published simultaneously in Canada by Fitzhenry and Whiteside, Markham, Ontario L3R 4T8

Library of Congress Cataloging-in-Publication Data
Ransom, Candice F., 1952–
The promise quilt/Candice F. Ransom; illustrations by Ellen Beier.
p. cm.
Summary: After her father leaves the family farm on Lost Mountain to be
General Lee's guide, Addie finds ways to remember him—even when he does
not return at the end of the war.
ISBN 0-8027-8694-4 (hardcover). —ISBN 0-8027-8695-2 (reinforced)
1. Virginia—History—Civil War, 1861–1865 Juvenile fiction.
[1. Virginia—History—Civil War, 1861–1865 Fiction. 2. United
States—History—Civil War, 1861–1865 Fiction. 3. Family life Fiction.]
I. Beier, Ellen, ill. II. Title.
PZ7.R1743Pr 1999
[Fic]—dc21   99-13053
                                            CIP

Book design by Diane Hobbing of Snap-Haus Graphics

Printed in Hong Kong

10 9 8 7 6 5 4 3 2 1